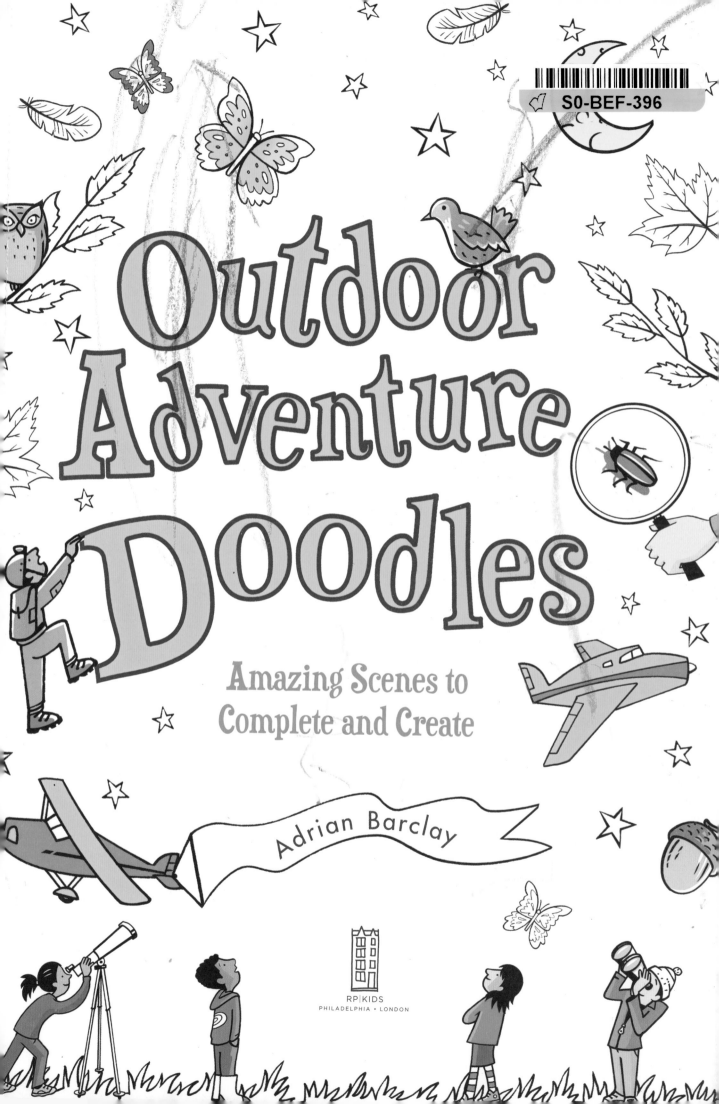

Outdoor Adventure Doodles

Amazing Scenes to Complete and Create

Adrian Barclay

RP|KIDS
PHILADELPHIA · LONDON

First produced in Great Britain in 2014 by Buster Books,
an imprint of Michael O'Mara Books Limited,
9 Lion Yard, Tremadoc Road, London SW4 7NQ.

First published in the United States by Running Press Book Publishers, 2014

Printed in China

Books published by Running Press are available at special discounts for bulk purchases in the
United States by corporations, institutions, and other organizations. For more information,
please contact the Special Markets Department at the Perseus Books Group, 2300 Chestnut
Street, Suite 200, Philadelphia, PA 19103, or call (800) 810-4145, ext. 5000, or e-mail
special.markets@perseusbooks.com.

ISBN 978-0-7624-5218-7

Illustrated by Adrian Barclay
Edited by Sophie Schrey
Designed by Jack Clucas

9 8 7 6 5 4 3 2 1
Digit on the right indicates the number of this printing

This edition published by:
Running Press Kids
An Imprint of Running Press Book Publishers
A Member of the Perseus Books Group
2300 Chestnut Street
Philadelphia, PA 19103–4371

Visit us on the web!
www.runningpress.com/kids

Design the ultimate tree house.

Doodle awesome designs on their parachutes.

Fill the bus with people
and pile stuff on the roof.

Complete the tracks
and draw the animals
that made them.

Give these backpacks
fun designs.

Build them
a shelter.

Add designs to the banners!

What have they found
on their fossil hunt?

What's in
the caves?

Doodle more ATVs, and spray mud everywhere!

Go kayak crazy!

Doodle more bats in the trees.

What have they caught?

What are they roasting on the fire?

Build amazing mud sculptures.

Finish the
ice-skating scene.

Outdoor party fun.

What are they crossing over?

Draw more vehicles in the traffic jam.

What's growing in the
vegetable garden?

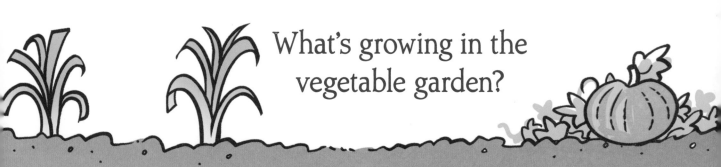

Draw more tents and
build a fire at basecamp.

Finish their picnic feast.

Doodle more cyclists.

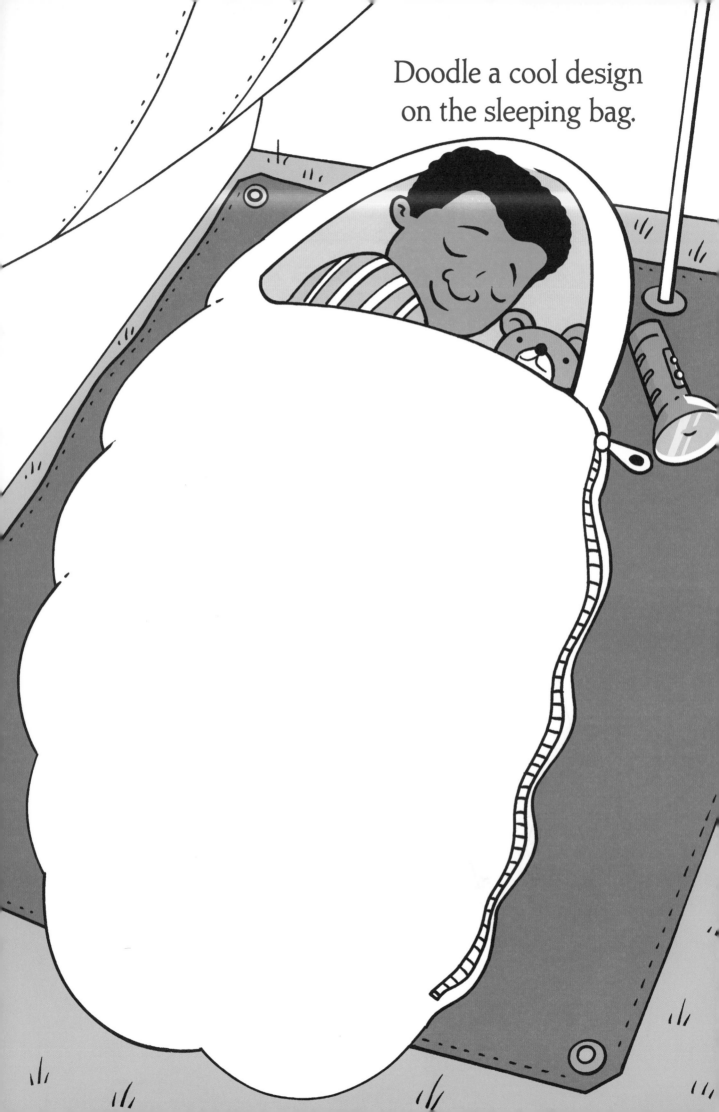

Doodle a cool design
on the sleeping bag.

Dreaming of an outdoor adventure . . .

Shhh! What has he discovered?

Doodle daring designs on the sails.

Draw more climbers.

Butterflies!

Arctic adventures!

The bees are
on the loose!

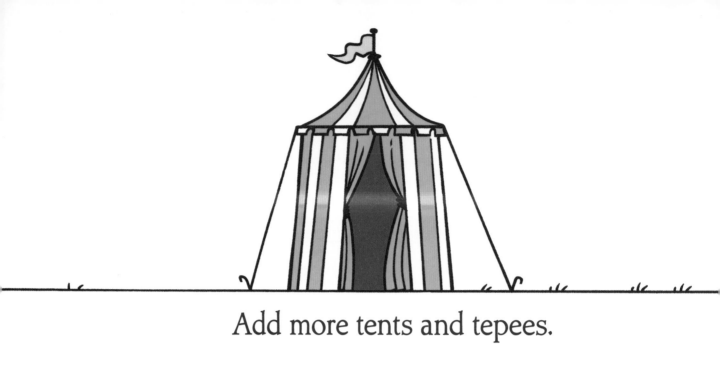

Add more tents and tepees.

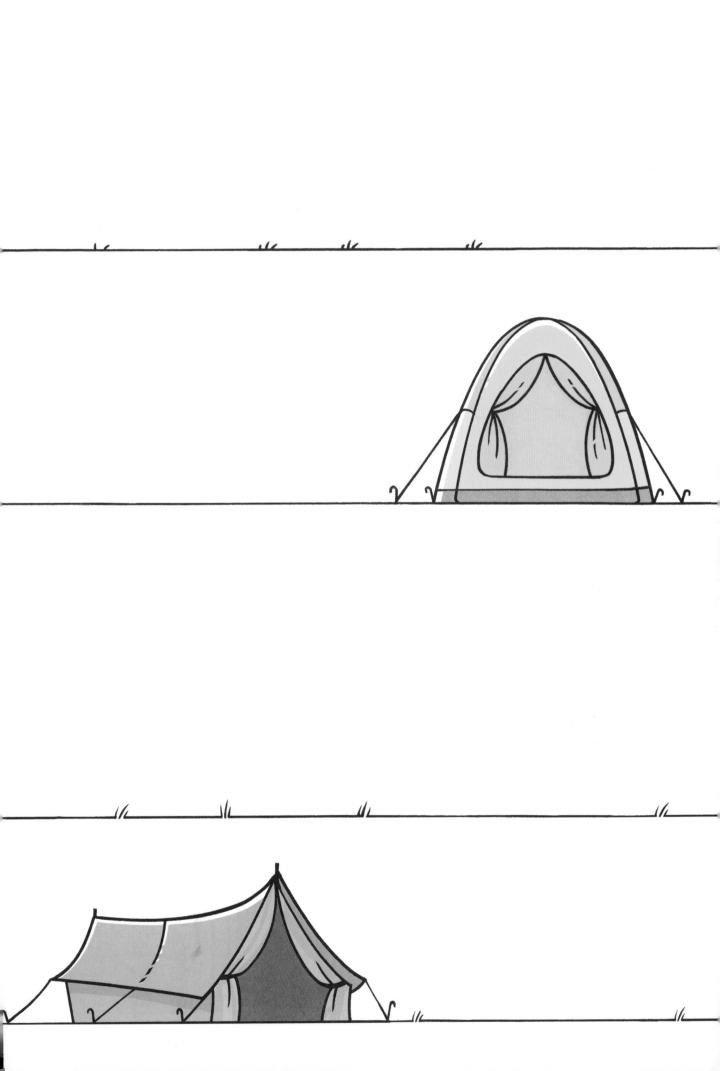

Bring the meadow to life with more flowers and insects.

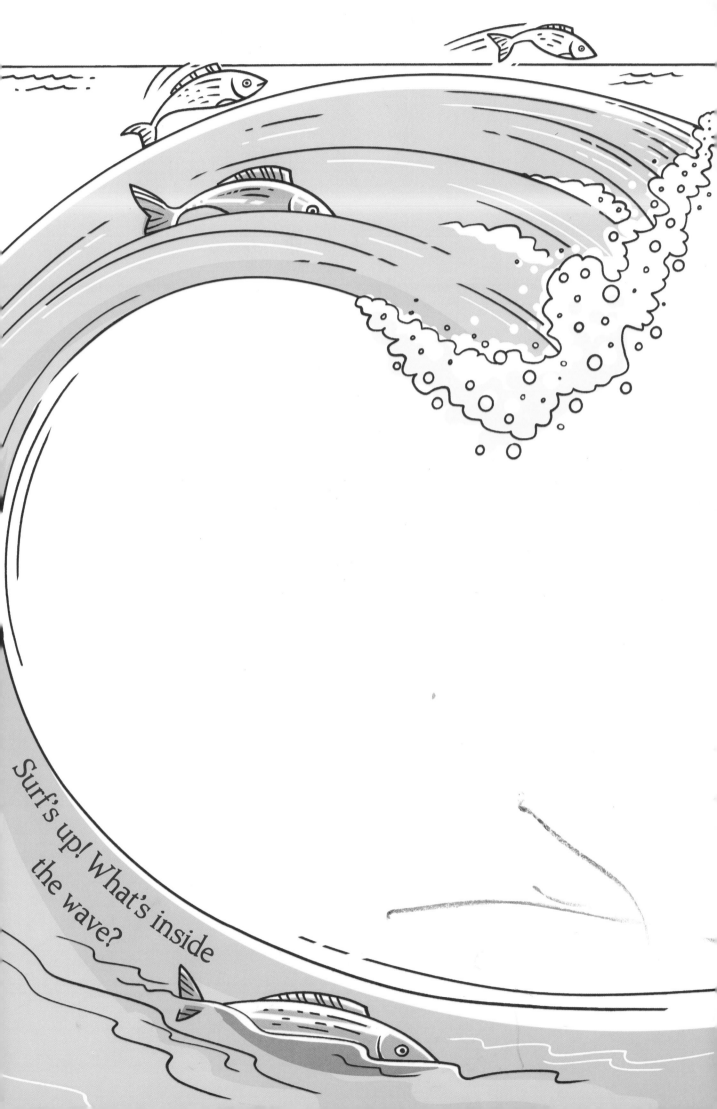

Surf's up! What's inside the wave?

Dress him for
a cold . . .

. . . and a hot adventure.

Draw the scenery you'll see on the zip line.

Delicious ice cream for weary hikers.

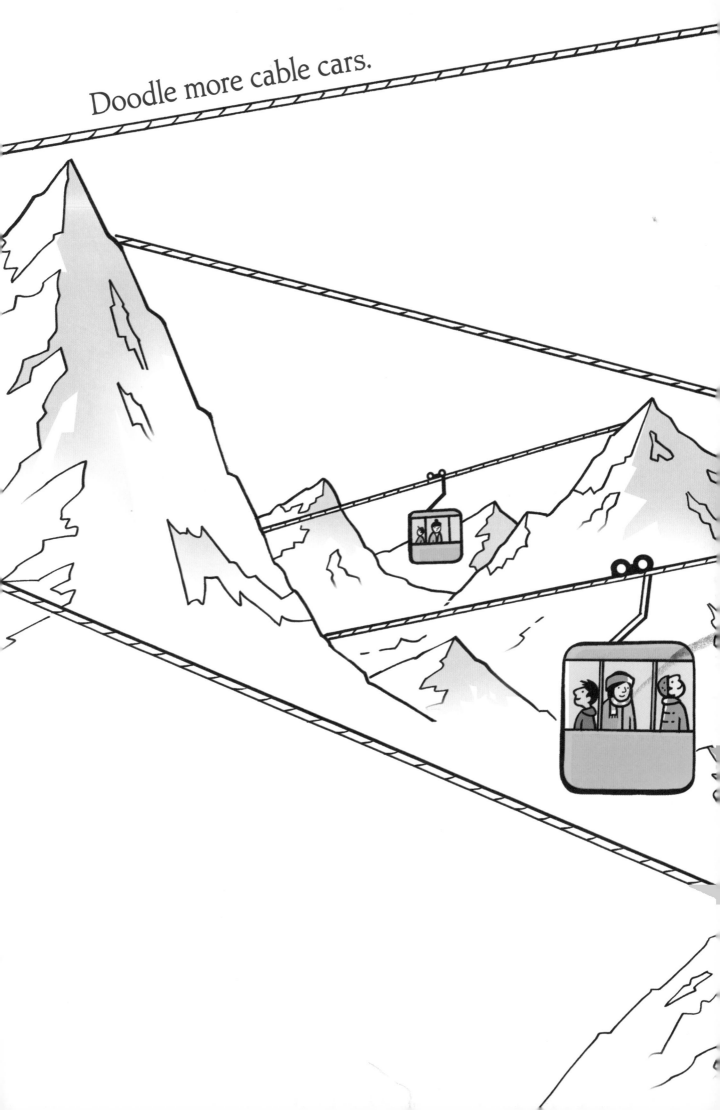
Doodle more cable cars.

What can you see through the binoculars?

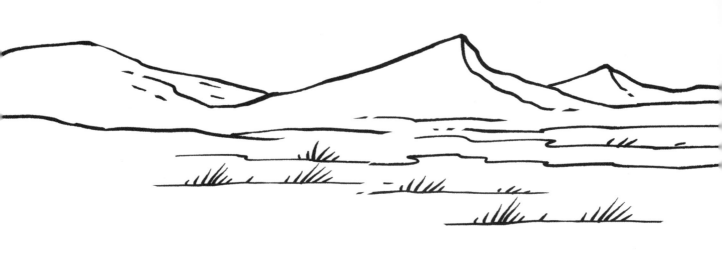

Doodle a
Western scene.

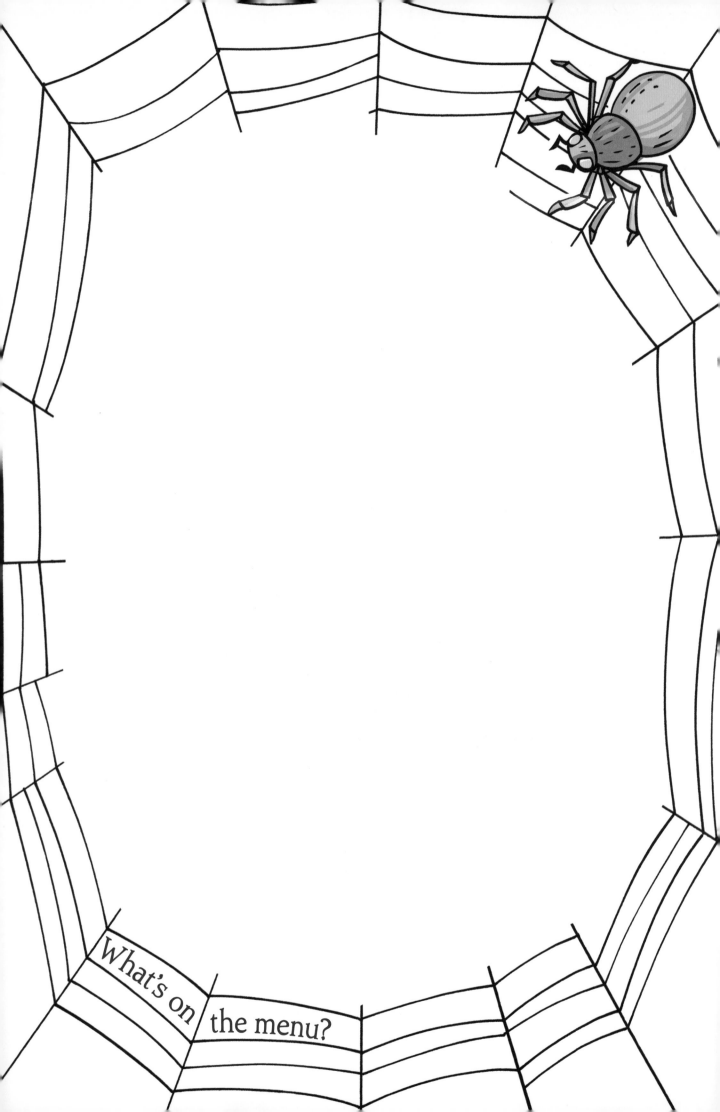

What's on the menu?

What are the skiers dodging?

Fill the sky with comets, planets, and stars.

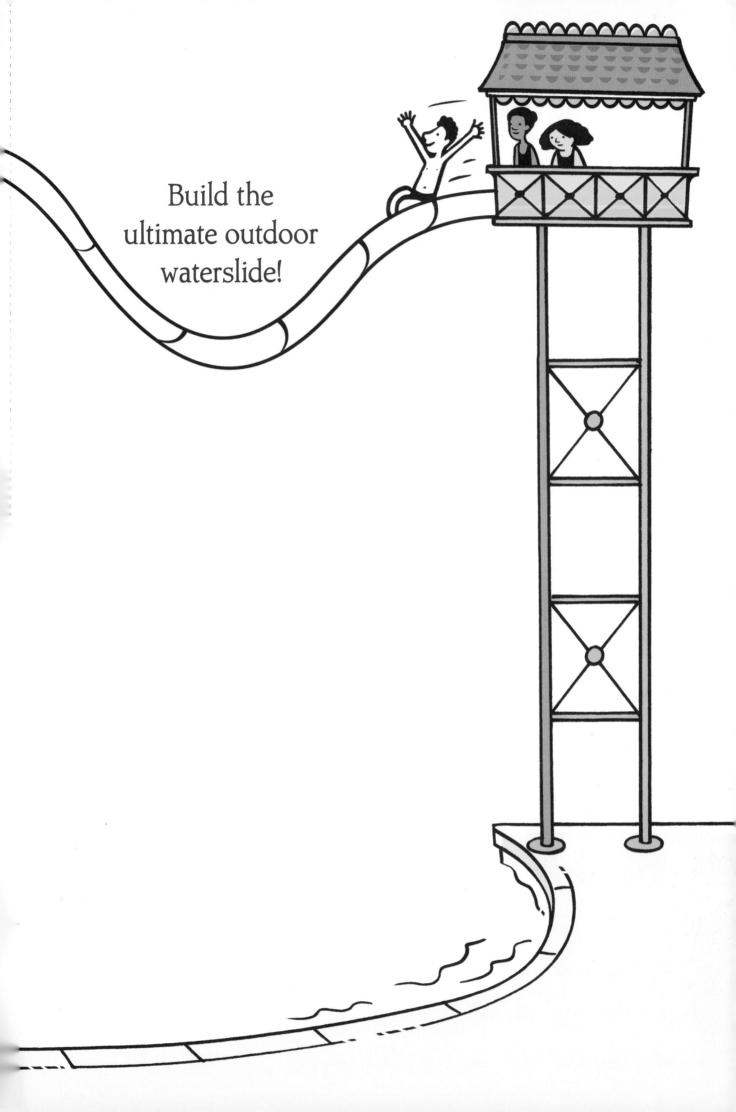

Build the
ultimate outdoor
waterslide!

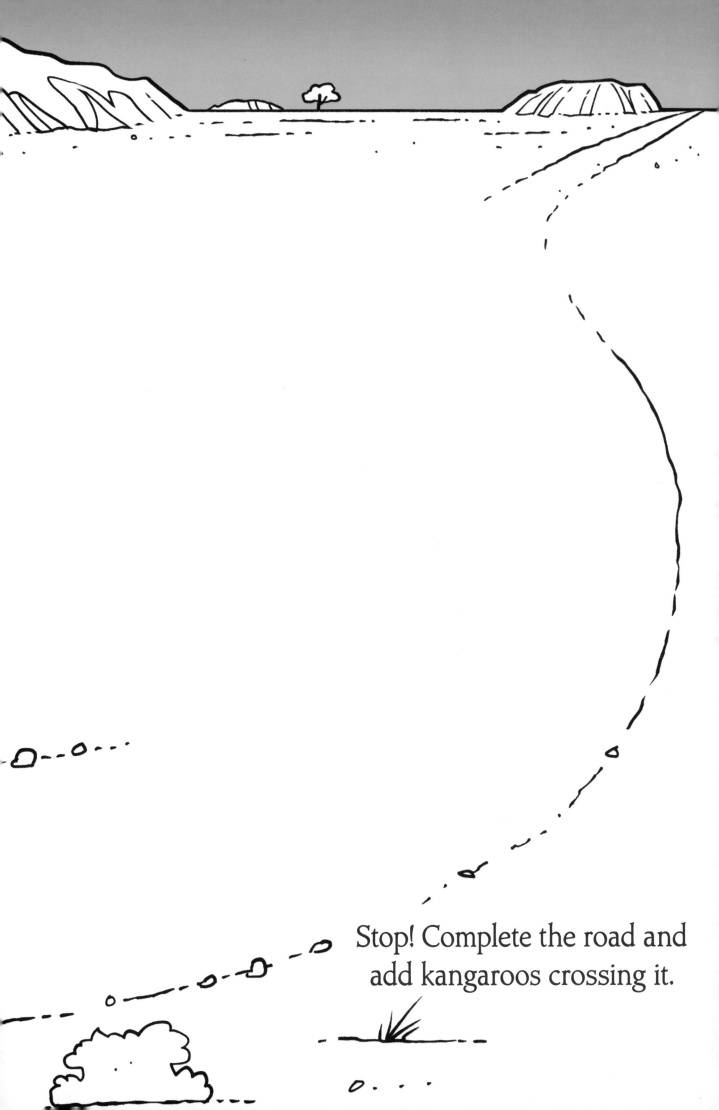

Stop! Complete the road and
add kangaroos crossing it.

What has the
eagle dropped?

Doodle more
safari silhouettes.

All aboard!

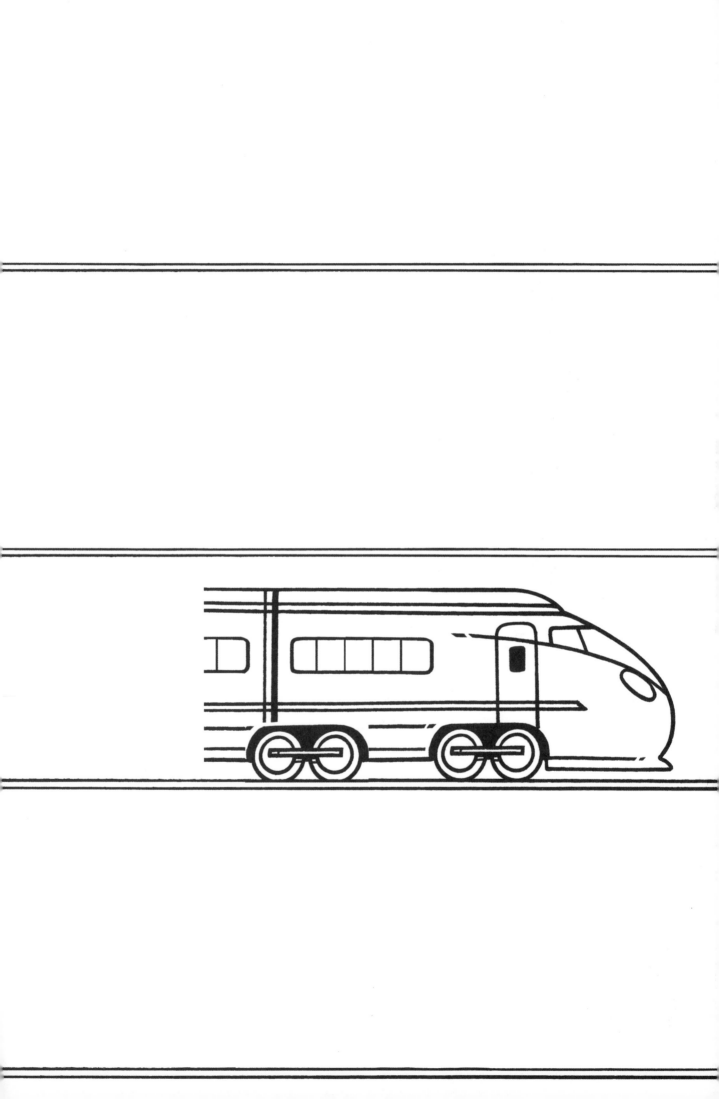

Doodle some
creepy-crawlies
close-up.

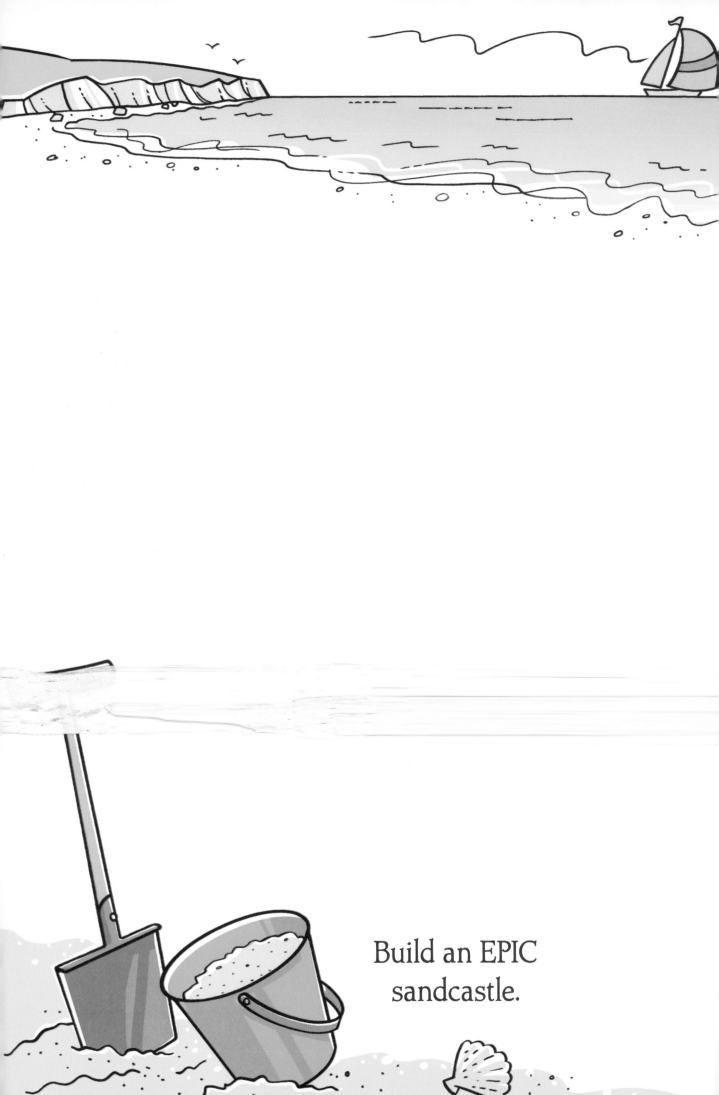

Build an EPIC
sandcastle.

Wow,
what a view!

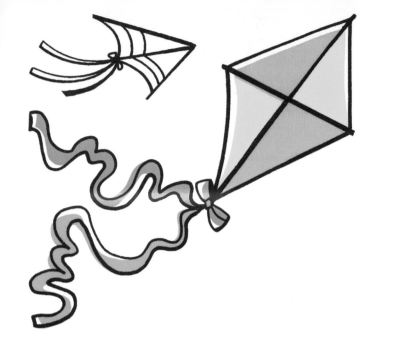

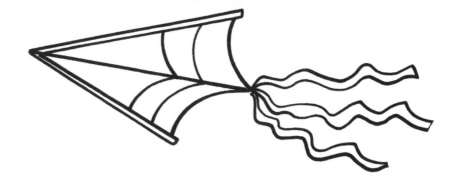

Cool kites on a windy day.

Arghh!

What does he see?

Fill the tree with nests and birds.

Fill the sky with hot air balloons!

Draw hungry
birds and bags
of nuts.

Draw more bouncing frogs.

Fill the city farm
with animals.

Doodle cool patterns on the campers.

What have they spotted?

What's under the microscope?

Build your dream mountain lodge.

What cloud shapes
are in the sky?

Sledding fun and
snowball fights!

Doodle **TOWERING**
trees and tiny people.

Give him a cool parachute!

BBQ time! What's cooking?

Where have you been?

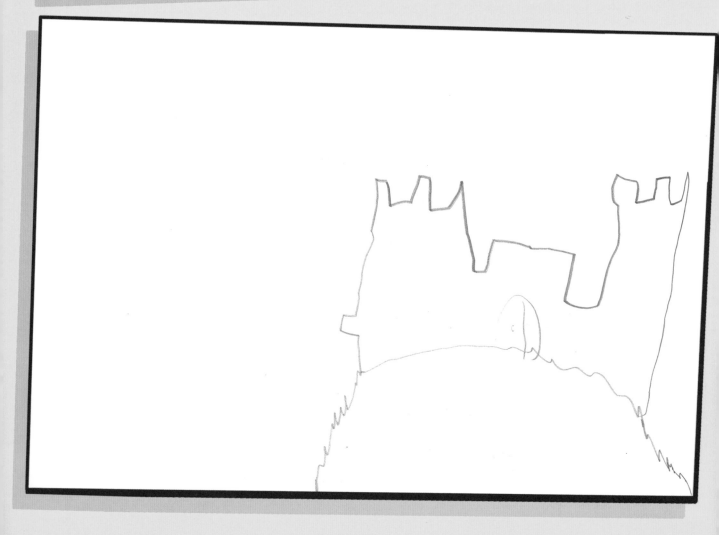

Time for an outdoor adventure!
What's in the trailer?

Hide-and-seek!
Doodle places to hide.

Draw more hikers
and their dogs.

What do the spelunkers see in the cave?

Complete the row
of beach huts.

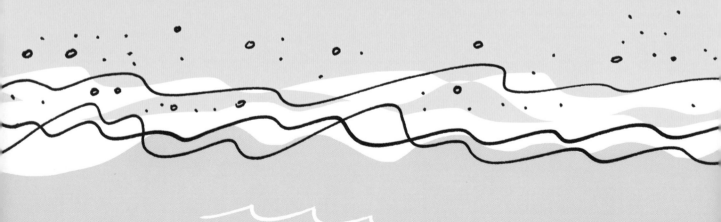

Build an awesome adventure playground.

Build them an
amazing campfire.

Crawling crabs
everywhere!

Plot your adventure . . .

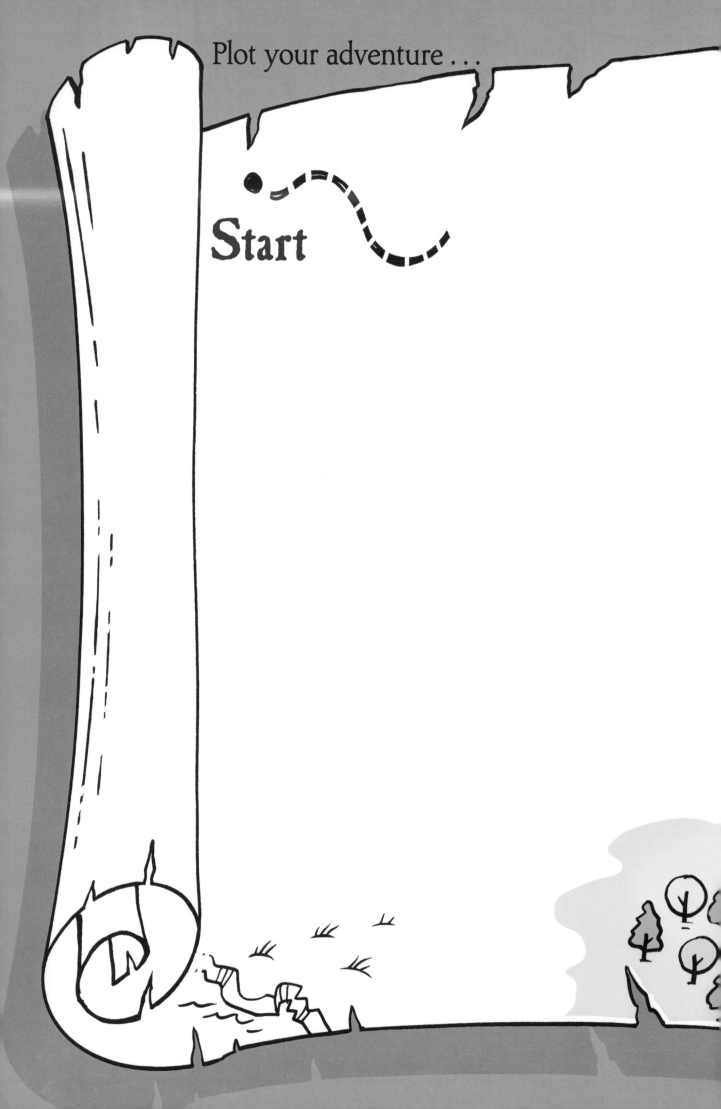

Start

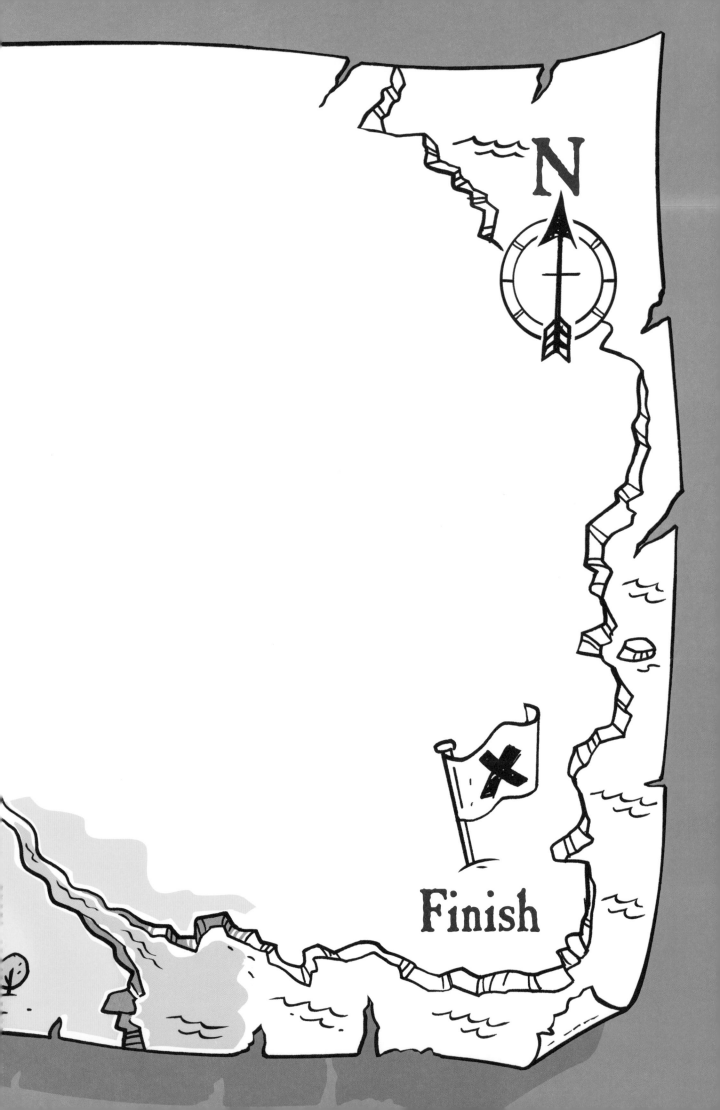

Doodle the reflection in the water.

Nature trail! What have you collected?

Pinecone

Acorn

Oak leaf

Add more mountain bikes.

What have they drawn in the sand?

Design your own stamps.

Draw ropes and bridges
for a treetop adventure.

QUICK! Build them a bridge.

Add more climbers
to the wall.

Make them a raft!

Give them a building
to rappel down.

What's in the woods?

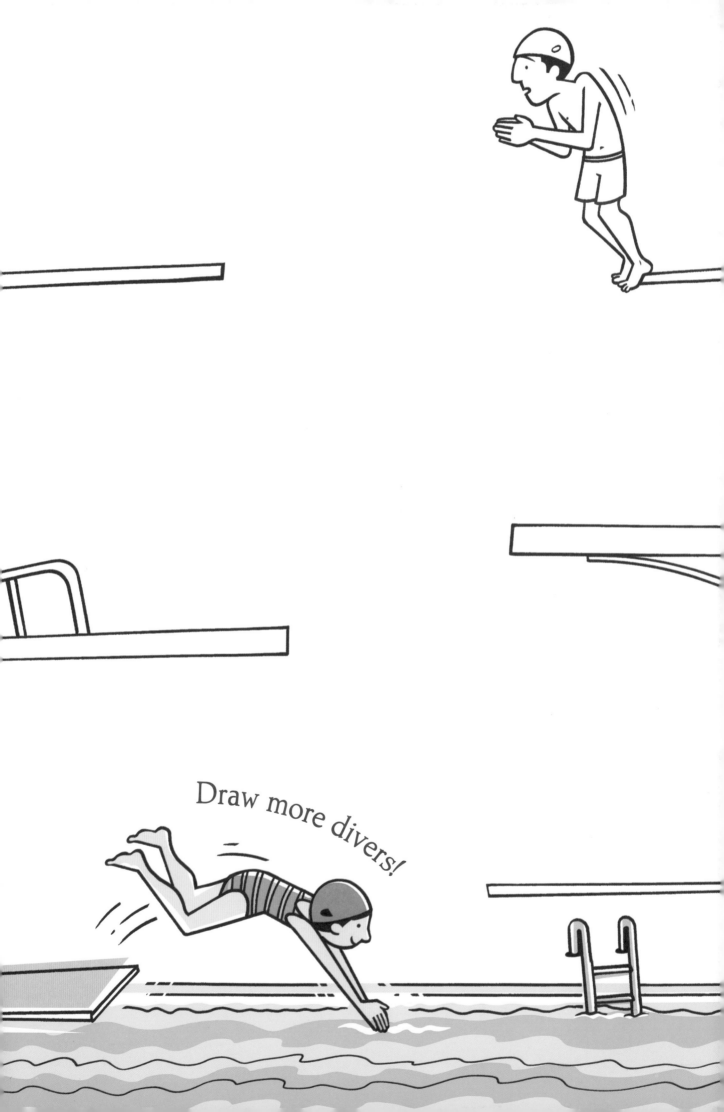

Draw more divers!

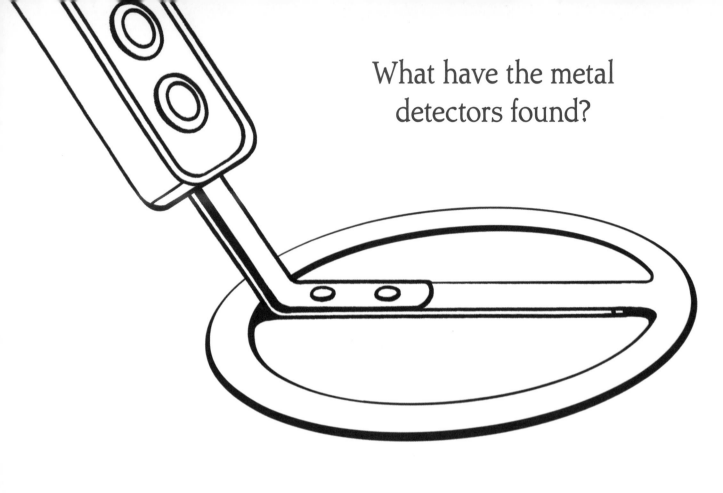

What have the metal
detectors found?

Complete the campsite.